SHRUBS
&
TREES

VRONI GORDON

Illustrations by
ELAINE FRANKS

This edition first published in 1997 by
Parragon
Units 13–17 Avonbridge Trading Estate
Atlantic Road, Avonmouth
Bristol BS11 9QD

Produced by
Robert Ditchfield Publishers

ISBN 0 75252 144 6

A copy of the British Library Cataloguing in Publication
Data is available from the Library.

Typeset by Action Typesetting Ltd, Gloucester
Colour origination by Colour Quest Graphic Services Ltd,
London E9
Printed and bound in Italy

"With thanks to **J**"

SYMBOLS

Where measurements are given, the first is the plant's height
followed by its spread.
The following symbols are also used in this book:

$\bigcirc$ = thrives best or only in full sun
$\mathbb{D}$ = thrives best or only in part-shade
$\bullet$ = succeeds in full shade
E = evergreen

Where no sun symbol and no reference to sun or shade is
made in the text, it can be assumed that the plant tolerates
sun or light shade.

POISONOUS PLANTS

Many plants are poisonous and it must be assumed that no
part of a plant should be eaten unless it is known that it is
edible.

CONTENTS

SHRUBS AND TREES

There is little need to ask why trees and shrubs are so important in our landscape and in our gardens. Because of their woody trunks and stems the hardy ones survive winters and can go on growing year after year and so they are our most constant and faithful companions. Their framework – even if they have lost their leaves – is still visible in the winter when most of the perennials, the colourful annuals and the bulbs have died down or been dug up, when even the grass may have disappeared under a blanket of snow.

Because they stay with us not only throughout the year but over many years, some becoming the largest plants of all, it is to trees and shrubs we turn to provide the permanent shape of the garden – to form the living 'walls' and the most important 'furniture'. They can be used as a background, but they can also star in their own right, giving us pleasure with their leaves, flowers, berries, hips, bark and scent. Yet again, whenever there is a special need – something to grow in a difficult spot, for instance – we can be sure that a plant can be found to meet it.

Being spoilt for choice, however, can be a mixed blessing when it comes to selecting plants. So often a visit to the garden centre will tempt us to buy something merely because of its pretty flowers without regard to anything else, and the flowers may well have faded before we have found a home for such an impulsive, perhaps already regretted, purchase. Far better, when planning a new garden or changing an established one, to look at the site first and think of what kind we need, what we want it to do for us, how it will fit in. Bearing this in mind, the

Opposite: A composition of colour and shape.

Rhododendron hybrids 'Golden Torch' and 'Sneezy' provide neat domes of brilliant colour.

chapters of this book have been arranged to describe some of the most important ways in which we use these varied and versatile plants.

Deciding on which trees and shrubs are most suitable becomes easier also if thought is given to some of the main characteristics (apart from flowers, dealt with in Chapter 2) which account for such a great diversity.

SHAPE AND HABIT

How trees and shrubs are best used depends so much on these. If there is need of a shady canopy to sit under on a lovely summer's day, it would quite obviously be foolish to cut down the old spreading apple tree and replace it with a typically pyramid-shaped conifer.

A flowery combination: the pink *Cistus* 'Peggy Sammons' surrounded by lilac trumpets of penstemon.

But there are many other shapes, and do we always consider them? Three different flowering cherries: one a slender upright column, the other a weeping tree and the third like an up- and outward-reaching vase. One of them makes a gentle accent, the other could look beautiful as a specimen in the lawn, the third would nicely preside at the back of a mixed border. Many shrubs form the familiar hummock, but there are others which arch, like the beauty bush (*Kolkwitzia amabilis*); which have a striking architectural appearance like the rhus; or which just spread on the ground – after all, the periwinkle and the ivy are shrubs too.

Habit can dictate where we plant our trees and shrubs. The bare trunks of some trees are especially beautiful and we make sure they can be seen; on the other hand, the leafless stems of a lilac or philadelphus are not very attractive and are best placed at the back of a border with other plants in front of them to act as petticoats.

LEAVES

The most obvious distinction relating to leaves is whether they all come off in the autumn or not – whether the plant is deciduous or evergreen – and the implications of this are equally obvious. Nonetheless, a few words of caution. For some purposes, such as hedging, ground cover, background planting, or even for providing a cheering sight out of the window on a dreary winter's day, the steady presence of evergreens is a distinct advantage; but the changing scene provided by deciduous plants is to be welcomed also – the fresh leaves as they emerge in spring, the glories of the autumn tints.

Leaf colour needs to be interesting but also restful. Greens can vary so much – from light to dark, from yellowish to bluish – and should not be overlooked as the most important of all the colours. There is a place for the delicate silvers and greys. Few of us can resist the exciting highlight of a bright yellow tree or shrub, or the beauty of a purple-leaved smoke tree, not to mention all the variegations, but they should always be used with discretion. Plants in a garden are not seen in isolation; they are part of a picture.

Less obvious than colour, but very important nonetheless, are the other ways in which leaves differ. They come in all shapes and sizes, from the needles of a pine to the almost plate-sized ones of a catalpa. The texture varies also, and this will affect how the plant looks. The smooth, polished leaves of a holly or choisya will reflect light and look shiny; the rough, sometimes hairy ones of a Hydrangea aspera do not, and so give quite a different impression.

The choice of tree and shrubs with variegated or golden foliage has lightened this border.

CULTURAL REQUIREMENTS

We have so far considered the qualities of plants which we take into account when we choose them to suit ourselves. But will these plants grow for us? Some can be quite particular as to the acidity or alkalinity of the soil, its quality and composition (clay, loam, sandy, chalk), whether it is well drained or not; they may need a spot which is shady or in full sun; they may tolerate salt winds or pollution or they may not.

The last two chapters of this book deal with trees and shrubs for very special conditions or with special needs, but it pays at all times to consider the plants' requirements and, of course, however tolerant they are, they should be planted and subsequently looked after with care.

1. SHRUBS AND TREES TO FORM THE GARDEN

PLANTING *the* BOUNDARIES

HEDGES COME FIRST TO MIND. They can vary from tall, narrow 'living walls', created by regular clipping of trees such as thuja, yew, holly, beech, hornbeam and hawthorn, to less formal wider barriers of shrubs, such as barberries.

Trees and shrubs when allowed to grow naturally on garden boundaries form excellent screens and windbreaks. Suitable for shelter belts are conifers such as the **Serbian spruce** (*Picea omorika*) and hardy deciduous trees such as the **whitebeam** (*Sorbus aria* **'Lutescens'**) shown here.

Creating *a* Framework

BOUNDARIES MERELY OUTLINE A GARDEN. By planting tall evergreen shrubs inside we can subdivide the usual rectangle into different areas, creating more interesting spaces not all seen at a glance.

Both straight lines and soft curves can be created with trees and shrubs. The promontory of taller plants here, forming a bay, is softened by lower foreground shrubs.

◆ *Internal hedges, of yew for instance, are well loved. Here conifers are used for a less formal structure.*

Illustrated here are some useful plants. ***Photinia × fraseri* 'Red Robin'** has attractive red new foliage and can reach 6 × 4m/20 × 13ft.

***Prunus lusitanica* (Portugal laurel)**, larger still, bears white flower spikes in early summer. ***Viburnum x burkwoodii* 'Park Farm Hybrid'** (3 × 2.4m/10 × 8ft) scents the garden throughout spring with its round white flower heads.

***Lavandula* 'Grappenhall'**
Frost hardy. Lavenders are
suitable for low hedges. Fragrant flowers mid/late summer. O, E, 1 × 1.5m/3 × 5ft

***Buxus sempervirens* (Box)** A
low hedge here but could be
2m/6ft or more. Fully hardy,
box grows in sun or deep
shade. E, 5 × 5m/16 × 16ft

***Artemisia* 'Powis Castle'**
Fine foliage shrub. Pruned
hard in spring, it quickly re-
grows. O, E, 1 × 1.2m/3 × 4ft

***Juniperus sabina*
'Tamariscifolia'** The Savin
juniper is valuable for dry
banks or border edges. E,
1 × 2m/3 × 6ft

***Santolina pinnata* ssp.
neapolitana (Cotton
lavender)** Ideal for edging
or mass planting. Yellow
flowers midsummer. O, E,.
75cm × 1m/2½ × 3ft

SMALLER GARDENS, as well as subdivided areas of larger ones, still need the permanent backbone planting of evergreens, not only as hedges or isolated groups. In a mixed border they give it shape and stability.

***Lonicera nitida* 'Baggesen's Gold'** Cheerful even in midwinter. The green form often used as hedging. E, 1.5 × 1.5m/5 × 5ft

***Escallonia* 'Apple Blossom'** For borders or hedges in mild areas. Flowers early to midsummer. Dark glossy leaves. ○, E, 2 × 2.4m/ 6 × 8ft

Euphorbia characias* subsp. *wulfenii Magnificent yellow-green flowers in spring. This spurge is effective on its own or in borders. E, 1 × 1m/3 × 3ft

***Brachyglottis* 'Sunshine'** (syn. *Senecio* 'Sunshine') Easily controlled shape, lovely foliage and yellow summer flowers. O, E, 1 × 1.5m/3 × 5ft

Rhus hirta (syn. *R. typhina*) Stag's-horn sumach renowned for its orange-red autumn foliage and interesting architectural shape. 5 × 6m/16 × 20ft

Sorbus vilmorinii Graceful small tree with delicate leaves turning orange and red in autumn. Pink fruits. 5 × 5m/16 × 16ft

Malus hupehensis Magnificent spring-flowering crab with deep green foliage and large scented white flowers. The crab apples that follow in autumn are yellow with a red tinge. 10m × 10m/33 × 33ft

SPECIMEN TREES

THESE FORM FOCAL POINTS within the framework and should have special qualities such as beautiful shape, flowers, foliage, bark or berries. Above all, their ultimate size must suit the setting.

Pyrus salicifolia **'Pendula'** Grey-leaved pear, mound-shaped and weeping. 7.5 × 7.5m/25 × 25ft

Acer griseum (**Paper-bark maple**) Beautiful peeling bark, autumn colours and shape – a most desirable maple. 8 × 6m/26 × 20ft

***Chusquea culeou* (Chilean bamboo)** Stout stems slowly form a large clump of strong, upward-thrusting shape. E, 5 × 2.4m/16 × 8ft

Fargesia nitida (syn. *Sinarundinaria n.*) Small leaves, white with frost here, usually mid-green. Purple-stemmed bamboo of indefinite spread. E, 5m/15ft

Yucca filamentosa Lanceolate mid-grey leaves and long-lasting white flowers on tall panicles. ○, E, 2 × 1.5m/6 × 5ft

***Phormium tenax* (New Zealand flax)** Sword-shaped leaves and panicles of bronze-red flowers. ○, E, 2.4 × 1.5m/8 × 5ft

SPECIMEN SHRUBS

PLANTED SINGLY ON A LAWN any shrub would catch our attention – a favourite rose, perhaps. But distinctive shape, habit or leaf interest are some of the outstanding features which turn others into focal points, whatever the setting.

Magnolia stellata (**Star magnolia**) White star-shaped flowers in early spring. Slow growing but most worthwhile. 3 × 4m/ 10 × 13ft

◆ *Plant magnolias where morning sun cannot damage frosted flowers.*

GOOD PARTNERS

DECIDUOUS SHRUBS, particularly those
rounded in shape, blend and mix well
if leaf colour is carefully considered.
Their foliage, changing with the
seasons, augments the more static
evergreens in borders.

Rosa **'Cornelia'** flowers all
summer. Ideal for mixed
borders. ◯, 1.2 × 1.2m/
4 × 4ft

◆ *Other valuable hybrid
musk roses are: 'Buff
Beauty' and 'Felicia'.*

***Cotinus coggygria* 'Royal Purple' (Smoke tree)**
Magnificent foliage turns bright red late autumn. Summer flowers. 4 × 4m/ 13 × 13ft

***Weigela florida* 'Foliis Purpureis'** Purple-green leaves and pink tubular flowers. 1.2 × 1.5m/ 4 × 5ft

***Cornus alba* 'Elegantissima'** This dogwood is normally a rounded bush but has been pruned here into a mop-head. 3 × 4m/10 × 13ft

***Spiraea* 'Arguta' (Bridal veil)** Gracefully arching with white spring flowers. Dainty leaves yellowing in autumn. 2.4 × 2.4m/8 × 8ft

GROUND COVER *in* SHADE

SOME PLANTS, mostly evergreen, form a leafy weed-suppressing cover, whether they are low carpeting or taller. Not only utilitarian, they have landscaping value also, the low ones providing quiet flat areas to set off other plants.

Mahonia aquifolium (Oregon grape) Not for dry soil. Has handsome glossy foliage, scented yellow spring flowers and autumn berries. E, 1 × 1.5m/3 × 5ft

Viburnum davidii has unusually bold, deeply veined leaves. The turquoise blue autumn berries are remarkable also. E, 90cm × 1.5m/3 × 5ft

Lonicera pileata Box-like leaves on low branches. Tolerates dry shade. E, 60cm × 2m/2 × 6ft.

Vinca minor **'Aureo-variegata'** Lesser periwinkles have white or purple flowers. Rapidly spreading trailers. E, 15cm/6in (spread indefinite)

Euonymus fortunei **'Emerald Gaiety'** Lively variegated foliage. Can climb or creep. E, 1 × 1.5m/3 × 5ft

Hedera helix **'Glacier'** The evergreen trailing shoots of ivy root as they spread, rapidly forming an attractive carpet.

Rhamnus alaternus **'Argenteovariegata'** This bushy buckthorn will tolerate semi-shade. E, 3 × 3m/10 × 10ft

***Hypericum calycinum* (Rose of Sharon)** Grows almost anywhere with yellow flowers throughout summer. However, can be invasive. E, 30cm/12in

***Hebe pinguifolia* 'Pagei'** has fine glaucous leaves and white spring flowers. Will sprawl into neglected corners. E, 30cm × 1m/ 1 × 3ft

***Rosa* 'Red Blanket'** Low shrub rose with glossy, healthy foliage, flowering repeatedly. 1.2 × 2m/4 × 6ft. 'Rosy Cushion' and 'Swany' are lower still and a light pink. 75 × 150cm/2½ × 5ft. Of easy maintenance as winter pruning can be done mechanically or with shears.

Erica carnea Easily maintained, these winter heaths will tolerate some lime and shade. E, 30 × 45cm/12 × 18in

◆ *Mulch heaths and heathers regularly with organic matter.*

GROUND COVER
in the OPEN

WHERE THE GARDEN needs a flat 'breathing space', lawns come first to mind. But they are far more labour intensive than some shrubs which not only fulfil the same function but are problem solvers for difficult positions such as steep banks and poor dry soil. Furthermore, the often interesting habit and colourful foliage of shrubs are valuable design and landscaping assets.

Juniperus horizontalis **'Wiltonii'**, sometimes called the Wilton carpet juniper or 'Blue Rug'. There are many creeping junipers, all hardy evergreens, loving sun and good drainage. Varying in growth rate and spread, their siting and spacing is important. Other cultivars include 'Bar Harbor', 'Douglasii', 'Plumosa', 'Blue Chip' and the Glauca group.

2. INTEREST THROUGH THE SEASONS

SPRING TREES

WE ARE SPOILT FOR CHOICE because so many trees have beautiful spring foliage and flowers. Some are too large, but others – particularly ornamental cherries, magnolias, crab apples and hawthorns, to name but a few – are suitable even for the smallest plot.

Sorbus aria 'Lutescens' The leaves of this whitebeam, silver-grey in spring, become green and white-backed later. 12 × 7m/ 39 × 23ft

Prunus 'Pink Shell' An elegant ornamental cherry for those who prefer delicate to strong pink flowers. 9 × 8m/30 × 26ft

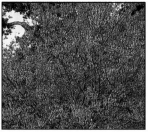

Cercis siliquastrum The Judas tree bears pink flowers late spring and red pods later. ○, 10 × 10m/ 33 × 33ft

Crataegus laevigata 'Paul's Scarlet' Hawthorn with masses of double red flowers late spring. Glossy foliage. 6 × 7m/20 × 23ft

SPRING SHRUBS

SHRUBS WHICH ARE HARDY IN COOL CLIMATES tend to flower at this time, their beauty transforming the garden after the long winter. Many of them, especially viburnums and daphnes, are wonderfully fragrant.

Salix lanata The woolly willow is a sturdy little shrub often planted in rockeries although, like most willows, it enjoys moist soil. 1 × 1m/3 × 3ft

◆ Salix hastata *'Wehrhahnii' has attractive catkins also. Those of the much larger shrub S.* gracilistyla *'Melanostachys' are black.*

Magnolia liliiflora **'Nigra'**
flowers from mid-spring to
midsummer. A beautiful,
hardy, aristocratic shrub. E,
4 × 3m/12 × 10ft

Viburnum × juddii produces
its sweetly scented flowers,
pink in bud, freely from
mid to late spring. 1.5 ×
1.5m/5 × 5ft

Chaenomeles speciosa
'Nivalis' A vigorous quince
whose flowers, continuing
throughout spring, are
followed by large yellow
fruits. A thorny shrub, taller
than *C. japonica*, it lends
itself to wall training, when
side shoots should be cut
back after flowering. 2.4 ×
5m/8 × 16ft

***Daphne odora* 'Aureo-marginata'** has very early fragrant flowers. A gem needing protection and some shade. E, 1.5 × 1.5/5 × 5ft

Daphne mezereum Scented flowers appear before leaves late winter/early spring. 1.2 × 1.2m/4 × 4ft

***Camellia* 'Rubescens Major'** An upward-growing, hardy japonica cultivar. Needs lime-free, humus-rich, cool, moist soil and protection. ◑, E, 3 × 3m/10 × 10ft

◆ *Camellias, beautiful all year, grow well in containers where conditions are easily controlled.*

Ribes sanguineum
'Brocklebankii', 'King
Edward IV' and
'Pulborough Scarlet' are
some favourite flowering
currants. 2 × 2m/6 × 6ft

Berberis darwinii Spiny
shrub for borders, mass
planting or hedges. Purple
berries in autumn. E,
4 × 4m/13 × 13ft

***Prunus tenella* 'Firehill'**
Resents pruning. *P. ×
cistena*, of similar size, has
purple leaves and white
flowers. O, 2 × 2m/6 × 6ft

Forsythia × intermedia
Useful for hedging. (Best
trimmed after early spring
flowering). 3 × 2m/10 × 6ft

Cytisus × kewensis. Low and
arching, for walls, rock
gardens or ground cover.
Light prune only. O, 45cm
× 1.5m/1½ × 5ft

The flowers of **Syringa vulgaris (common lilac)** cultivars are unsurpassed. Other lilacs may be preferred for elegance. ○, 6 × 4m/20 × 13ft

Deutzia × elegantissima 'Rosealind' Beautiful shrub, as are white-flowered deutzias such as *D. gracilis.* 1 × 1.5m/3 × 5ft

Ceanothus 'Blue Mound' A beautiful shrub which needs shelter as it is not fully hardy. ○, E, 1.5 × 2m/5 × 6ft

◆ *Bold plants like this stand out well against paving or fussy backgrounds.*

EARLY SUMMER

THE GARDEN IS IN FULL SWING NOW with hostas and hardy geraniums at the feet of our shrubs, irises and peonies beside them. A time for many pinks and blues – softer than the vibrant colours of high summer – and the fresh green of shrubs and trees now in full leaf.

'Graham Thomas' An English rose, which resembles the Old roses but flowers all summer. ○, 1.2 × 1.2m/4 × 4ft.

'Fritz Nobis' A vigorous, early-flowering Modern shrub rose related to *R. rubiginosa*. ○, 2 × 1.5m/6 × 5ft

ROSES

Roses have been unchallenged favourites for centuries. Species roses and their close relatives are the first to flower. They are hardy shrubs which, needing little pruning, can develop their natural beautiful habit, shape, flowers, foliage and often hips.

Among those out in early summer: *Rosa moyesii*, *R. xanthina* 'Canary Bird', *R.* 'Nevada', the 'Frühlings' (spring) roses, *R. rugosa*. The Old French roses will start soon with Hybrid Teas, Floribundas, English roses and many more to follow.

Philadelphus **'Belle Etoile'** One of the best mock oranges, this arching shrub is smaller than *P.* 'Virginal', taller than *P.* 'Manteau d'Hermine'. Abundantly produced white flowers have purple blotches at the base. ○, 2.4 × 2.4m/8 × 8ft

Exochorda × *macrantha* **'The Bride'** Needs pruning immediately after flowering. ○, 2.4 × 3m/8 × 10ft

Paeonia delavayi **var. ludlowii** formerly *P. lutea l.* It is the largest tree peony with beautiful bright green foliage. ○, 2.4 × 2.4m/8 × 8ft

This laburnum tunnel gives height, shade and restricted visibility. For smaller gardens, pergolas, covered in climbers, will do the same, taking even less room.

◆ *For maximum effect underplant laburnums with bulbs or herbaceous plants that flower at the same time.*

MID-SUMMER

AT THIS TIME the shrubs which were hard pruned in spring come into their own. They include *Buddleja davidii* (butterfly bush), some clematis, deciduous ceanothus, roses and lavateras. For the valuable shrubby potentillas, hypericums and helianthemums this is but part of a long flowering season.

Lavatera **'Barnsley'**, given full sun and well-drained soil, will flower for months. Valuable even though not very hardy. Take cuttings as insurance. 2 × 1m/6 × 3ft

◆ Abutilon × suntense, *flowering somewhat earlier, also not fully hardy, is another fast-growing shrub easily propagated.*

Genista aetnensis, the Mount Etna broom, presides over this border of blue and yellow flowers. Also yellow-flowered but much smaller (1.2 × 1.2m/ 4 × 4ft) is the versatile shrub *Hypericum* **'Hidcote'**. Light blue *Ceanothus* × *delileanus* **'Gloire de Versailles'** is complemented by the lower-growing lavender (*Lavandula angustifolia* **'Hidcote')** which, like the hypericum, is named after a famous garden. Sprawling over its neighbours, the indigo *Clematis* × *durandii* is a cross between a shrubby and a herbaceous species.

LATE SUMMER FLOWERS

SOME OF THE MOST VALUABLE SHRUBS for late summer are the long-flowering kinds like potentilla and hypericum, which begin earlier in the summer. But it is the hydrangeas and fuchsias that are probably the most popular at this time. Most hydrangeas retain their flowers into autumn.

Buddleja davidii This beautiful, fast-growing shrub flowers best if hard pruned in spring. Popular and widely naturalized in the West now, it originally came from China, discovered there in 1869. 4 × 4m/13 × 13ft

***Fuchsia* 'Margaret'** Hardy fuchsia in bloom from late summer till the frosts. Cut stems to base in spring. 1.2 × 1m/4 × 3ft

Hydrangea villosa Spectacular lace-cap blooms. Prefers semi-shade and acid soil but will tolerate lime. 2.4 × 2m/8 × 6ft

Potentilla fruticosa Generously flowers all summer. Most useful shrub for ground cover, borders or banks. 1.2 × 1.2m/4 × 4ft

***Hypericum* 'Rowallane'** Semi-evergreen and frost hardy, it will flower from mid-summer to late autumn. 1.5 × 1.5m/5 × 5ft

Caryopteris* × *clandonensis Pruned to ground level each spring, grows quickly. Late, valuable blue flowers. ○, 80 × 80cm/2¹/₂ × 2¹/₂ft

Leycesteria formosa Also requires drastic spring pruning. The flowers are followed by shining purple fruits. 2 × 2m/6 × 6ft

***Viburnum opulus*
'Xanthocarpum'** Fast-growing and hardy. White lace-cap flowers followed by translucent berries. 4.5 × 4.5m/15 × 15ft

***Malus* 'Everest'** Pink-white flowers smother this dwarf crab apple in spring. Suitable for small gardens. 3.6 × 2.4,m/12 × 8ft

***Cotoneaster frigidus*
'Cornubia'** Semi-evergreen ideal screening shrub. Weighed down by its berries in autumn. 7 × 7m/23 × 23ft

***Pyracantha* (Firethorn)** Suitable for hedges and walls even in shade. Long-lasting berries. E, 4 × 3m/13 × 10ft

***Callicarpa bodinieri* var.
*geraldii*** Autumn brings purple foliage and these remarkable berries. 4 × 4m/13 × 13ft

Autumn Fruit

Many shrubs and trees make their greatest impact when smothered in fruits or berries. The cotoneasters and pyracanthas are perhaps the most impressive, but even plants grown mainly for their flowers like roses, crab apples and viburnums will brighten the garden with autumn fruits. Birds will share the feast of course, but do we really mind?

***Cornus kousa* (Chinese dogwood)**. An elegant shrub. These fruits follow a wonderful summer display of white 'flowers'.
7 × 5m/23 × 16ft

♦ *The flowers of dogwoods are themselves small but are set off by petal-like bracts.*

AUTUMN TINTS

THE FALL, so aptly named, brings with it one of the great spectacles of the year when nature's very own bonfire sets the dying leaves aflame. Our gardens, too, have their star performers, particularly the acers and sumachs.

***Rhus glabra* 'Laciniata'**
3 × 3m/10 × 10ft is a tough, wide shrub smaller than ***Rhus hirta***. Both sumachs excel in the autumn.

◆ *Sumachs sucker freely. When pruning, beware of the irritating sap.*

Euonymus alatus slowly growing to 3 × 3m/10 × 10ft is best planted singly to show off its spreading habit.

The maple-like leaves of ***Liquidambar styraciflua*** appear only in late spring or early summer.
16 × 8m/52 × 26ft

This corner is half-shaded by *Malus tschonoskii*, one of the best crabs for autumn colour. *Acer palmatum* **'Osakazuki'**, on the right, displays its fine leaves and shape against the background of *Rosa rugosa* **'Alba'** which has turned a soft yellow. To the left, versatile *Amelanchier* **'Ballerina'** adds vibrant oranges and reds whilst *Hydrangea serrata* **'Preziosa'**, at their feet, tries to calm the scene with its more sombre purple tints.

***Viburnum × bodnantense*
'Dawn'** A very frost-resistant shrub with small fragrant flowers. 3.5 × 3.5m/12 × 12ft

***Viburnum tinus* 'Eve Price'**
The pink flowers of this valuable shrub defy the frost from autumn to spring. E, 2.4 × 2.4m/8 × 8ft

Hamamelis mollis The Chinese Witch Hazel, its spidery flowers richly scented. 5 × 6m/16 × 20ft

Garrya elliptica A bushy shrub which welcomes wall protection. The magnificent catkins last for many weeks. E, 4 × 3m/13 × 10ft

Mahonia japonica A great architectural shrub with lax, lily of the valley-scented flowers. E, 3.5m × 3m/ 12 × 10ft

WINTER FLOWERS
and BARK

MANY PLANTS flower at this time and we
become more aware of the bark on trees.

Betula utilis var. ***jacquemontii*** Ghostly white stems and a
snowy, peeling trunk give this birch an outstanding
presence. It has a broader outline than *Betula albosinensis*
which would be preferable where space is limited. 15 ×
7m/49 × 23ft

3. SHRUBS AND TREES FOR SPECIAL PLACES

THIN SOIL *over* CHALK

THESE ARE DIFFICULT CONDITIONS which few plants prefer though many will tolerate.

Purple-leaved *Weigela florida* **'Foliis Purpureis'** is a slow-growing deciduous shrub rarely exceeding 1.2 × 1.5m/4 × 5ft. Its tubular pink flowers appear in late spring, early summer, as do the larger flower panicles belonging to the lilac *Syringa* **'Antoine Buchner'**, an upright shrub – to 4m/13ft. Shown below is a branch of *Cotoneaster horizontalis* whose leaves turn red in autumn when the shrub is bedecked with bright red berries.

DAMP SITES

MANY MORE PLANTS than those illustrated here thrive in damp (though not water-logged) soil, including alders and poplars among trees, neillia and symphoricarpus among shrubs, as well as bamboos.

Salix alba vitellina **'Britzensis'** This willow has been pollarded to keep it small. The new stems are bright red and make an attractive feature.

Sorbaria tomentosa **var.** ***angustifolia*** (syn. ***aitchisonii***) Flowers last midsummer to autumn. Prefers sun. 3 × 3m/ 10 × 10ft

Cornus alba Versatile shrubs grown for foliage and/or bright red winter stems. Often hard-pruned. 3 × 3m/10 × 10ft

Sambucus racemosa **'Plumosa Aurea'** Elder with outstanding yellow foliage if hard-pruned in spring, otherwise 3 × 3m/10 × 10ft.

HOT DRY PLACES

WHERE PLANTS ORIGINALLY COME FROM often explains their likes and dislikes. Hot dry conditions suit many whose natural habitat is near the Mediterranean or in countries with similar climates.

***Cistus* 'Elma'** A sturdy bush with exceptionally large flowers in summer. The rock or sun roses do well on chalk and hate being transplanted. E, 2 × 2m/6 × 6ft

◆ *Cistus and helianthemum are both commonly known as rock or sun roses.*

Rosmarinus officinalis
Aromatic foliage shrub
flowering late spring/early
summer. Has culinary and
ornamental uses. E,
1.5 × 1.5m/5 × 5ft

Lupinus arboreus The tree
lupin is a vigorous
sprawling fairly short-lived
shrub flowering in early
summer. Semi-E,
1.5 × 1.5m/5 × 5ft

Lavandula Lavenders, for
border fronts or low hedges,
are much loved for scented
flowers and foliage. E,
1 × 1m/3 × 3ft

**Helianthemum 'Golden
Queen'** Many rock roses are
fully hardy, flowering late
spring to autumn. E, 30cm
× 1m/1 × 3ft

Convolvulus cneorum has
silky silvery leaves and
blush-white funnel-type
flowers. Tenderish and
needs shelter. E, 60 × 60cm/
2 × 2ft

HEAVY SHADE

THESE PLANTS share a tolerance of deep shade though they do not necessarily prefer it.

Sarcococca hookeriana **var.**
digyna Deliciously scented
winter flowers are followed
by black fruits. Prefers leafy
open soil. E, 1 × 1m/3 × 3ft

× *Fatshedera lizei* Grand
foliage and interesting
flowers best in moist soil.
Can be trained up walls,
etc. E, 2 × 3m/6 × 10ft

Elaeagnus pungens
'Dicksonii' A framework
shrub smaller than *E. p.*
'Maculata'. E, 2.4 × 3m/8 ×
10ft

Fatsia japonica Large-
leaved, prefers moist soil.
Impressive and fast-
growing. E, 3 × 3m/10 ×
10ft

4. SHRUBS AND TREES WITH SPECIAL NEEDS

LIME-FREE SOIL

THE SO-CALLED 'LIME-HATERS' (or calcifuges) are plants which become malnourished and cannot thrive in alkaline soil: that is, soil high in calcium. Ericaceous plants like heathers belong in this group and so do some others.

Kalmia latifolia **'Nimuck Red Bud'** produces beautiful spring flowers a few years after planting. Full sun, moist rich soil. E, 3 × 3m/10 × 10ft

Erica vagans **'Lyonesse'** flowers midsummer/ autumn. It is very intolerant of drought. O, E, 75 × 75cm/2½ × 2½ft

Fothergilla major Fragrant spring flowers and vivid orange-scarlet autumn foliage. 3 × 3m/10 × 10ft

RHODODENDRONS

RHODODENDRONS (WHICH INCLUDE AZALEAS) constitute a vast genus of flowering shrubs. Mostly hardy and otherwise not difficult to grow, they must be planted in neutral to acid soil, preferably well-drained and rich in humus.

R. Hybrid 'Bric-a-Brac'
Flowers late winter/early spring. Flowers are vulnerable to frosts outside. E, 1.5 × 1.5m/5 × 5ft

R. Hybrid 'Lem's Cameo'
The flowers, pink in bud, appear mid-spring. Needs extra care and shelter. E, 2 × 2m/6 × 6ft

R. Azalea 'Hino-mayo' Very floriferous, this evergreen forms a compact bush covered by small flowers in late spring. Tolerant of sun, it can be grown in containers for patio or conservatory use as well as in the garden. E, 1.5 × 1.5m/5 × 5ft

Central to the picture are the great blood-red flowers (7.5cm/3in across) of the evergreen Hybrid 'Elizabeth' which slowly grows to 1.2m/4ft.

Above, on the left, are the remarkable flowers of the exceptionally hardy Hybrid 'Peeping Tom', a dwarf evergreen which flowers in mid to late spring.

The white flowers on the right belong to Azalea 'Palestrina', a floriferous and hardy evergreen growing to 1.2m/4ft, flowering late spring.

The pink flowers (bottom left) are a close-up of *R.* Azalea 'Hino-mayo' featured in the lower photograph, whilst on the right is pink *R. yakushimanum*, an outstanding semi-dwarf species, evergreen and of compact habit, 1 × 1.5m/ 3 × 5ft.

IN NEED *of* WARMTH

THESE PLANTS ARE NOT HARDY below
–10°C/14°F, or in some cases below
–5°C/23°F. In colder gardens they
should be placed in a sunny sheltered
spot or grown up against a heat-
retaining wall.

Carpenteria californica Bright green glossy foliage perfectly
displays the white fragrant flowers in midsummer. E,
1.5 × 1.5m/5 × 5ft

◆ *If damaged by frost, carpenterias regenerate from old wood, even
if cut back to ground level.*

***Cistus* 'Peggy Sammons'** A lovely combination of grey-green foliage and a succession of pink summer flowers. E, 1.2 × 1.2m/ 4 × 4ft

***Cytisus battandieri* (Moroccan broom)** Has midsummer, scented flowers and silken, silvery leaves. Semi-E 5 × 5m/16 × 16ft

***Myrtus communis* (Common myrtle)** Aromatic foliage shrub with fragrant flowers followed by black berries. Excellent for seaside. E, 3 × 3m/10 × 10ft

***Ceanothus* 'Concha'** This Californian lilac has small leaves and intensely blue spring flowers. E, 2 × 3m/ 6 × 10ft

***Abelia* 'Edward Goucher'** Arching shrub with fragrant late-summer flowers. Semi-E, 1.5 × 1.5m/5 × 5ft

Itea ilicifolia The delicate drooping flower tassels are produced in late summer/early autumn. E, 3 × 3m/10 × 10ft

Cornus kousa bears small flowers surrounded by large bracts for a long period in early summer. 7 × 5m/ 23 × 16ft

Hydrangea anomala ssp. *petiolaris*. Very hardy climbing or groundcover plant for all soil and sun/shade conditions. 1 × 15m/3 × 49ft

Acer palmatum var. *dissectum* Best in dappled shade and protected from spring frosts. The form shown here is 'Atropurpureum'. 1.5 × 2.4m/5 × 8ft

Eucryphia × *nymansensis* Magnificent late-summer flowering tree. Needs its roots shaded and protection from cold winds. E, 15 × 4m/49 × 13ft

IN NEED *of* SHELTER *and* SOME SHADE

THE ANCESTORS OF MOST PLANTS HERE were woodlanders, so they have much in common, such as needing shelter from cold winds. However, they differ as to why and when they require shade. Acers, for instance, need protection from sun at mid-day whilst camellias in flower are vulnerable to early morning sun if they have been frosted overnight.

Camellia '**Konronkoku**' (syn. *C.* '**Kouron-jura**') Medium-sized shrub with particularly frost-resistant semi-double flowers. E, 2 × 2m/6 × 6ft

INDEX OF PLANTS